Brown v. Board of Education

Rachel Tisdale

PowerKiDS press™

New York

Published in 2014 by The Rosen Publishing Group
29 East 21st Street, New York, NY 10010

Produced for Rosen by Calcium Creative Ltd
Editor for Calcium Creative Ltd: Sarah Eason
US Editor: Joshua Shadowens
Designer: Paul Myerscough

Picture credits: Cover: Library of Congress: Warren K. Leffler. Inside: Corbis: Bettmann 15, 18, 20, 21, 23; Flickr: Keith Wondra 13; Library of Congress: 4, 29, George Grantham Bain Collection 7, Jack Delano 14, Detroit Publishing Co. 3, 16, Warren K. Leffler 24, 25, Thomas J. O'Halloran 22, Sun/Al Ravenna 1, Tolson & Schonberg 8, Marion S. Trikosko 27, Underwood & Underwood 11; National Park Service: 28; Robert Russa Moton Museum: Taylor Dabney 19; Shutterstock: Maximus256 12, Cameron Whitman 17; Wikimedia Commons: Library of Congress, Cornelius M. Battey 10t, Francis Bicknell Carpenter 5, Library of Congress 6, 10b, Skywriter 9, Cecil W. Stoughton, White House Press Office 26.

Library of Congress Cataloging-in-Publication Data

Tisdale, Rachel , author.
 Brown v. Board of Education / by Rachel Tisdale.
     pages cm. — (We shall overcome)
 Includes index.
 ISBN 978-1-4777-6073-4 (library) — ISBN 978-1-4777-6074-1 (pbk.) —
 ISBN 978-1-4777-6075-8 (6-pack)
 1. Segregation in education—Law and legislation—United States—
Juvenile literature. I. Title.
 KF4155.Z9T57 2014
 344.73'0798—dc23

                         2013028575

Manufactured in the United States of America

CPSIA Compliance Information: Batch #W14PK5: For Further Information contact Rosen Publishing, New York, New York at 1-800-237-9932

Contents

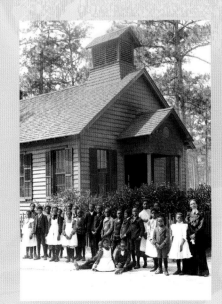

Slavery in the United States

For almost 250 years, white people forced Africans to be slaves in America. These African American slaves were forced to work, and they led hard and often brutal lives.

Tobacco, Cotton, and Sugar

In Virginia and North Carolina, European settlers grew tobacco to sell to Europe. By 1750, around 145,000 enslaved Africans worked on tobacco plantations. During the 1800s, demand for cotton and sugar grew, and huge plantations of these crops spread across the South. Thousands of African Americans worked on the plantations, some in the fields. Others worked as slaves to the plantation owners, catering for their every need. By 1860, there were 4 million slaves in the United States, more than half of which worked on plantations.

Many African Americans were forced to work on plantations, such as this cotton plantation in Georgia.

PICKING COTTON ON A GEORGIA PLANTATION.

Hope for Slaves

By 1865, slavery had been made illegal in the United States. For many slaves, it was a time to celebrate. Now they were free men, women, and children, and they hoped for a brighter future. However, in the South, where most of the former slaves lived and worked, white Americans were afraid of what life would be like when the former slaves mixed with them. They decided to take action to keep whites and African Americans apart.

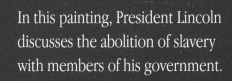

In this painting, President Lincoln discusses the abolition of slavery with members of his government.

Abraham Lincoln

Abraham Lincoln was born in a log cabin in Hardin County, Kentucky, in 1809. He taught himself law and went on to practice it, representing bankers and businessmen. Lincoln entered the world of politics, and in 1860, became the first Republican president to pledge to keep slavery out of the territories. Lincoln was shot on April 14, 1865, at Ford's Theater in Washington, D.C. Lincoln died the following day on April 15, 1865.

Segregation

The leaders in the southern states decided to make new laws to keep African Americans separate from white Americans. This became known as segregation.

Jim Crow Laws

The laws that the southern states passed were called Jim Crow laws. African American children had to go to separate schools and often had to walk long distances to and from school. White children, by comparison, caught school buses. African Americans had to eat in separate restaurants, sit on different seats on public transport, and even drink from separate public drinking fountains.

This African American man is drinking from the "colored" drinking fountain in a streetcar terminal in Oklahoma City.

In the North

While African Americans were suffering segregation in the South, life in the North was slightly better. At the start of World War I, there was a huge demand for workers in munitions factories. Some African Americans left the South and found work in northern cities, such as Chicago and New York. These cities developed large African American communities.

African Americans who moved north enjoyed being part of a freer community. Here, veterans from the American Civil War take part in a march in New York City.

Ku Klux Klan

Some white soldiers who fought in the American Civil War (1861–1865) wanted slavery to continue. After the war was over, these soldiers began to form organizations to intimidate African Americans. The largest of these organizations was the Ku Klux Klan (KKK). Its members wore white sheets, masks, and hats. They tortured, terrorized, and murdered African Americans.

"The Klan is inflicting summary vengeance on the colored citizens... by breaking into their houses at the dead of night, dragging them from their beds, torturing them in the most inhuman manner, and, in many instances, murdering."

Grand Jury investigation into the KKK in 1870.

Testing the Laws

The American Constitution guarantees every American citizen equal rights, but Jim Crow laws treated African Americans as second-class citizens. In 1891, a group called the Citizens Committee formed in New Orleans to test a new segregation law called the Separate Car Act.

Homer Plessy

On June 7, 1892, Homer Plessy took a seat in the white section of a railroad car on the East Louisiana Railroad Company train. Plessy was light-skinned because he was seven-eighths Caucasian and one-eighth African American. Nevertheless, he was asked to move from his seat. When he refused, Plessy was arrested, removed from the train, and taken to jail.

WARNING
No One Allowed On
THIS BRIDGE

The Separate Car Act stated that African Americans must sit in separate carriages to whites on Louisiana trains.

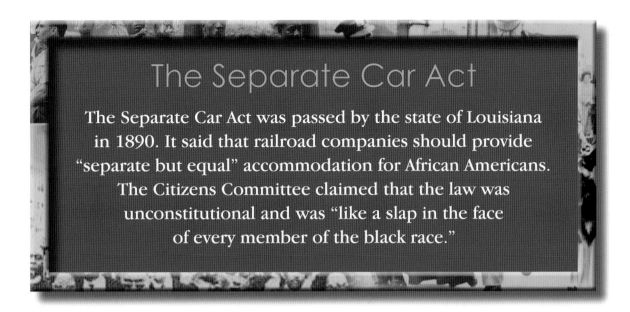

The Separate Car Act

The Separate Car Act was passed by the state of Louisiana in 1890. It said that railroad companies should provide "separate but equal" accommodation for African Americans. The Citizens Committee claimed that the law was unconstitutional and was "like a slap in the face of every member of the black race."

To Court

Plessy's lawyer argued that the Separate Car Act broke the Thirteenth and Fourteenth Amendments to the Constitution. The Thirteenth made slavery illegal, and the Fourteenth said no state can deny citizens of the United States equal protection of the laws.

Plessy was found guilty by the district court. The case was then taken to the US Supreme Court, where the judges ruled that racially separate facilities, if equal, did not violate the Constitution.

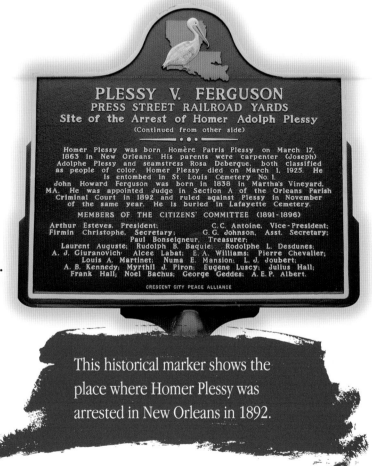

This historical marker shows the place where Homer Plessy was arrested in New Orleans in 1892.

African Americans faced violence, discrimination, and humiliation in almost every aspect of their lives. Even so, some did acquire a good education, and they and others formed organizations to fight for their civil rights. W.E.B. Du Bois was one such person.

W.E.B. Du Bois

After graduating from Fisk University, Du Bois taught at a number of colleges and became an active civil rights campaigner. In 1909, he joined other African and white Americans in New York City to form the National Negro Committee. The name of the organization was later changed to the National Association for

W.E.B. Du Bois (above) went on to edit the monthly NAACP magazine, *The Crisis* (left). The magazine was a voice through which African Americans could describe the unfair treatment they faced.

the Advancement of Colored People (NAACP). Its aim was to fight against racial injustice.

Peaceful Protest

The NAACP believed strongly in using only nonviolent forms of protest and legal action to bring about equal rights for African American citizens.

In 1917, in New York City, 8,000 African Americans marched in a silent protest against violence in the South.

Charles Houston

Charles Hamilton Houston worked as a lawyer for the NAACP and fought many of the organization's early cases against segregation in education. Houston argued that states that practiced segregation could not afford to maintain African American schools that were actually equal to those for whites. From 1935 to 1940, Houston successfully argued several cases using this strategy, including *Murray v. Maryland*, in 1936, which resulted in the desegregation of the University of Maryland's Law School.

THE FIRST BLOOD FOR AMERICAN INDEPENDENCE Was Shed By A Negro CRISPUS ATTUCKS

In the state of Kansas, a law passed in 1879 allowed segregated elementary schools in certain cities. In 1950, the NAACP division in Kansas set out to challenge this law.

Testing the System

In the city of Topeka, the NAACP gathered a group of 13 parents who agreed to bring a lawsuit on behalf of their 20 children. After seeking advice from professional lawyers, the parents attempted to enroll their children in segregated, "white only" schools. All the children were refused entry into the schools.

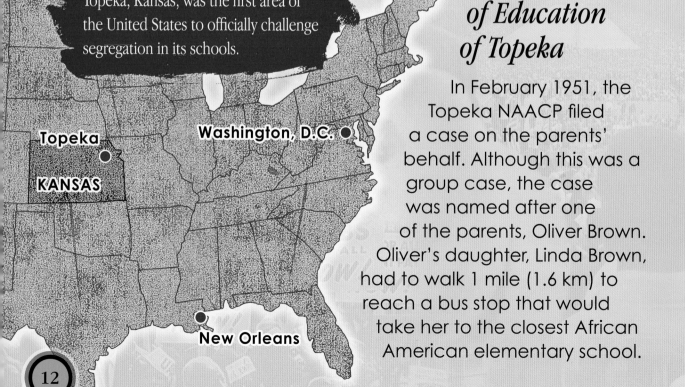

Topeka, Kansas, was the first area of the United States to officially challenge segregation in its schools.

Topeka

KANSAS

Washington, D.C.

New Orleans

Brown v. Board of Education of Topeka

In February 1951, the Topeka NAACP filed a case on the parents' behalf. Although this was a group case, the case was named after one of the parents, Oliver Brown. Oliver's daughter, Linda Brown, had to walk 1 mile (1.6 km) to reach a bus stop that would take her to the closest African American elementary school.

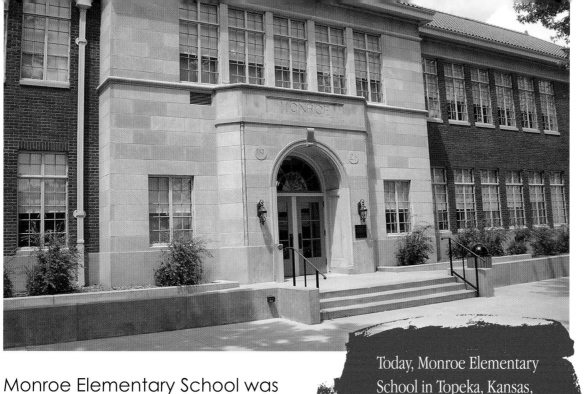

Monroe Elementary School was nearer to where Linda lived, just seven blocks away. Her father tried to enroll her in this school, but Linda was refused entry.

Today, Monroe Elementary School in Topeka, Kansas, is a historic landmark.

Multiple Cases

The legal team at the NAACP came up with a plan to challenge segregation. It was to involve more than one parent in each lawsuit, so that the courts could see there were many people all over the country who were not happy about the unequal facilities and education available to African American children.

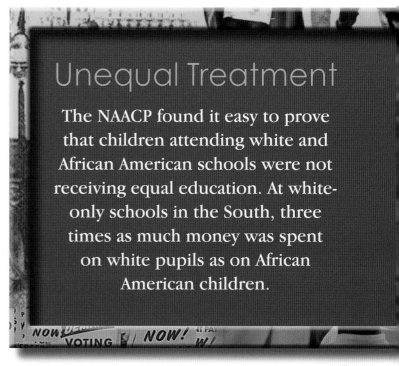

Unequal Treatment

The NAACP found it easy to prove that children attending white and African American schools were not receiving equal education. At white-only schools in the South, three times as much money was spent on white pupils as on African American children.

Brown v. Board of Education

On June 25, 1951, the *Brown v. Board of Education of Topeka* case came before the US District Court for the District of Kansas. At the trial, the NAACP argued that segregated schools were not "separate but equal."

Not Equal

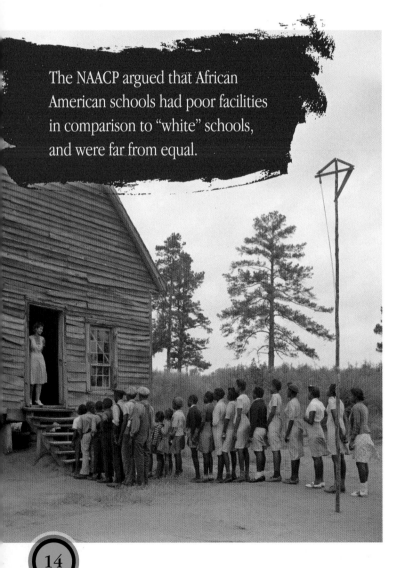

The NAACP argued that African American schools had poor facilities in comparison to "white" schools, and were far from equal.

It was argued by the NAACP that schools for African Americans did not provide equal facilities compared to schools for white children. In Topeka, there were 18 neighborhood schools for white children, while African American children had access to only four schools. This meant that it was impossible for many African Americans to attend schools that were nearby. The NAACP said segregation sent the message to African American children that they were inferior to whites and, therefore, the schools were naturally unequal.

The Court's Decision

Dr. Speer was the Chairman of the Department of Education at the University of Kansas City. He agreed with the NAACP's findings that African American schools were not equal to those of whites. Despite this, the district court ruled in favor of the school board of Topeka. The US District Court found that the physical facilities in white and black schools were comparable. They said "no willful, intentional, or substantial discrimination" existed in Topeka's schools. The parents and children felt defeated, but the NAACP did not give up. They decided to appeal the decision to the US Supreme Court.

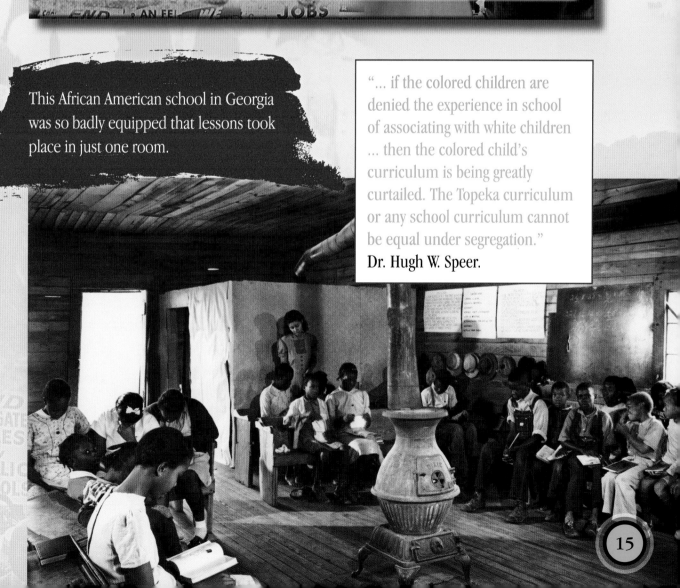

This African American school in Georgia was so badly equipped that lessons took place in just one room.

"... if the colored children are denied the experience in school of associating with white children ... then the colored child's curriculum is being greatly curtailed. The Topeka curriculum or any school curriculum cannot be equal under segregation."
Dr. Hugh W. Speer.

Delaware and South Carolina

Three further cases were brought before the courts to challenge segregation in schools, two in Delaware and one in South Carolina. Each case was known by the name of one of the parents versus the name of a member of the board of education.

Two Cases in Delaware

Instead of attending their local school, African American children in Claymont were forced to travel to a run-down high school 10 miles (16 km) away. Their case was called *Belton v. Gebhart*. Meanwhile in Hockessin, Sarah Bulah was frustrated because a bus for white children passed her house twice a day but would not pick up her daughter. Her case was called *Bulah v. Gebhart*. In 1951, with help from a local lawyer, the parents tried to enroll their children at the local white schools, but all the children were denied entry.

Many African Americans, such as these children at Pinehurst school in Summerville, South Carolina, traveled miles (km) each day to their school.

Victory in Delaware

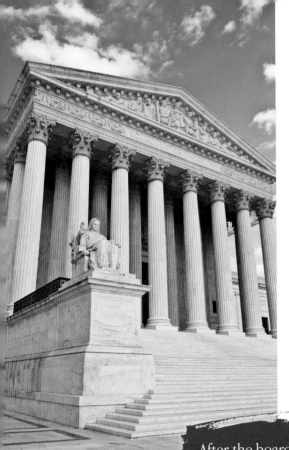

Both cases were taken to the Delaware Court of Chancery, where a ground-breaking decision was made. The chancellor ruled that the plaintiffs were being denied equal protection of the law and ordered that the 11 children involved be immediately admitted to the white school. It seemed a victory for the parents and children, until the board appealed to the US Supreme Court to overrule the decision.

After the board appealed the Delaware Court decision, the two cases joined others challenging segregation at the US Supreme Court.

Briggs v. Elliott

In South Carolina, 20 parents brought a case against R. W. Elliott, the president of the school board for Clarendon County. At first, the parents' requested only that the county provide school buses for their African American children. When their requests were denied, the NAACP helped them file a case that challenged segregation itself. At the US District Court, the judge refused the parent's request to end school segregation. However, the court did rule that the school board should begin equalization of schools.

District of Columbia and Virginia

Meanwhile, in the District of Columbia and the state of Virginia, African American parents and students were also demanding better school facilities. The cases challenged not only the idea of "separate but equal," but segregation itself.

District of Columbia

In the District of Columbia, African American Gardner Bishop was very unhappy with the poor standard of schools. He tried to enroll 11 African American students into the brand new Sousa High School in Washington, D.C. Even though the school had room for more students, the African Americans were refused entry.

Spottswood Bolling Jr., seen here with his mother, was one of the children Bishop tried to enroll at Sousa High School.

Challenging Segregation Itself

Bishop turned to NAACP lawyer Charles Houston to help him request a school building for African American children that was equal to Sousa High School. Houston asked his friend James Nabrit Jr. to represent Bishop and the students. Nabrit decided not to push for equal facilities, but to challenge segregation itself. It was a risky move. The *Bolling* v. *Sharpe* case was heard at the US District Court in 1951 but was unsuccessful.

Change in Virginia

Robert Russa Moton High School was one of only a few high schools available to African Americans in the state of Virginia. The school was desperately in need of repair, with temporary classrooms made out of tar-covered paper. In 1951, more than 100 students took part in a great strike to demand a new school building. They gained the support of the NAACP, and the case went to court. The US District Court ordered that the students be provided with equal school facilities but not access to the white schools in their area.

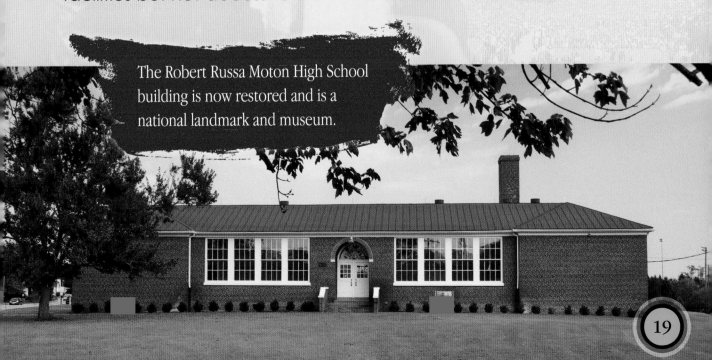

The Robert Russa Moton High School building is now restored and is a national landmark and museum.

US Supreme Court

By December 1952, cases from four states and the District of Columbia had been filed with the US Supreme Court, all of which challenged segregation in schools. They were the cases from Kansas, Delaware, South Carolina, Virginia, and the District of Columbia.

Combined Cases

The Supreme Court decided that it was best to hear the cases as one combined case, so that experiences of segregation in schools across the country would be examined together. The case was named *Oliver Brown v. the Board of Education of Topeka.*

The Supreme Court's decision to end school segregation made newspaper headlines.

Some of the attorneys who fought the *Brown v. Board of Education* case were George Hayes (left), Thurgood Marshall (center), and James Nabrit Jr. (right).

A Decision Is Made

When the Supreme Court first heard the case in December 1952, it failed to reach a decision. A year later, the Court examined the case again, and the effect of segregation on public education.

Success at Last

Eventually, the US Supreme Court ruled on May 17, 1954, that segregation in schools was unconstitutional. This was a huge success, not only for the parents and their children, but also for the NAACP, other civil rights organizations, and all African Americans in the United States.

"Does segregation of children in public schools solely on the basis of race, even though the physical facilities and other "tangible" factors may be equal, deprive the children of the minority group of equal educational opportunities? We believe that it does."

Chief Justice Warren reading the US Supreme Court's decision in *Brown v. Board of Education*.

After the Decision

Although the *Brown v. Board of Education* decision ended segregation in schools, it took a long time for many schools to integrate successfully. Even when African American children were finally allowed to attend the same schools as white children, many faced tough challenges.

Clinton, Tennessee

Two years after the Brown decision, Clinton High School in Tennessee was due to integrate. On August 27, 1956, 12 African Americans walked to the high school and attended class for the first time, without incident. The second day was different. The students faced threats, violence, and a large angry crowd. The violence escalated over the following week, and the police force was unable to cope. The National Guard were called in to calm the situation.

In Clinton, Tennessee, the National Guard were ordered to control school integration.

Little Rock Nine

It was a similar story in Little Rock, Arkansas. In 1957, nine African American students attempted to attend Little Rock Central High School. The governor of the state, Orval Faubus, was against the integration of the school, however, and called in the National Guard to block the students' entry. The event caught the nation's attention, and President Eisenhower intervened. He sent soldiers to help the students get to class. While it was a victory that the children were at school, they faced abuse on a daily basis.

Gaining Acceptance

A few people in Clinton who were against integration continued to protest, but the majority supported integration. When Bobby Cain graduated from Clinton High School in 1957, he became the first African American to graduate from an integrated school in the South.

Students Jefferson Thomas (center) and Elizabeth Eckford (right) were among those who integrated at Little Rock Central High School.

Changing History

The success of the *Brown v. Board of Education* case encouraged many civil rights organizations to push for equality in other areas of daily life, including public transport, restaurants, and jobs.

Students Come Together

Students throughout the South took part in "Freedom Rides," which tested desegregation on buses and facilities at bus stations. Buses were bombed, and students were badly beaten and thrown in jail during the rides.

Even some politicians remained opposed to integration. In 1963, Governor George Wallace tried to stop integration at the University of Alabama by blocking the entrance.

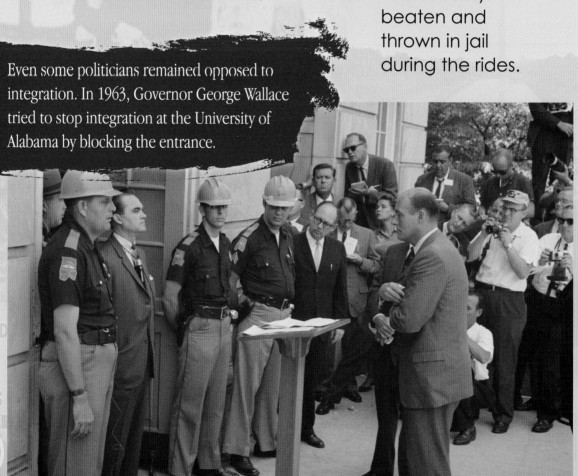

Civil rights leaders joined protesters taking part in the March on Washington for Jobs and Freedom in 1963.

Peaceful Sit-Ins

African American and white students opposed to segregation took seats that were reserved for white customers at lunch counters across the United States. When the African Americans were refused service, they continued to sit peacefully until the stores closed. After many months, department stores all over the country began to desegregate their lunch counters.

A Mass March

In August 1963, in Washington, D.C., hundreds of thousands of Americans took part in a peaceful march in support of equal jobs and freedom for all. The protesters listened intently to important leaders of the civil rights movement. Then Martin Luther King Jr. took to the podium and delivered his famous "I Have a Dream" speech. It was a momentous day for civil rights.

"I have a dream that my four little children will one day live in a nation where they will not be judged by the color of their skin, but by the content of their character."
Martin Luther King Jr.

25

The Civil Rights Act

At the time of the March on Washington for Jobs and Freedom, President John F. Kennedy was putting through a civil rights bill in government. When the president was assassinated just a few months after the march, many African Americans wondered if the bill would ever be made law.

President Lyndon B. Johnson

Kennedy's successor, Lyndon B. Johnson, made sure the civil rights bill became law, as an honor to the late President Kennedy.

"It is wrong, deadly wrong, to deny any of your fellow Americans the right to vote in this country." President Johnson, speaking to Congress.

Jackie Kennedy witnessed the inauguration of Lyndon B. Johnson as President of the United States.

Despite opposition from other congressmen, on July 2, 1964, President Johnson signed the Civil Rights Act. The Act stated that all public places and facilities must be desegregated. It also guaranteed African Americans the right to jobs.

Promise of Change

The new laws promised equality for all African Americans, but it took time for things to change. There were still outbreaks of violence, bombings, and even deaths in the southern states. Slowly, however, life changed for the better. African American children went to school with white children, and their future began to look brighter.

Voting Rights Act

A year after the Civil Rights Act, in 1965, Johnson signed the Voting Rights Act. The Act gave all African Americans the right to vote, outlawing the literacy tests and taxes southern states had forced African Americans to take and pay in order to vote.

Despite sweeping change, violence against African Americans continued for some time. This is the bomb-damaged house of an NAACP lawyer in Birmingham, Alabama.

A Lasting Legacy

The story of *Brown v. Board of Education*, which ended legal segregation in public schools, is one of hope and courage.

Children Today

Throughout the United States, today all American children can catch a bus to school and enjoy the right to an education with good facilities, teachers, and school buildings. This is all possible thanks to people who fought for their beliefs and convictions. Because of the people involved in the *Brown v. Board of Education* case, children today can look forward to a bright future.

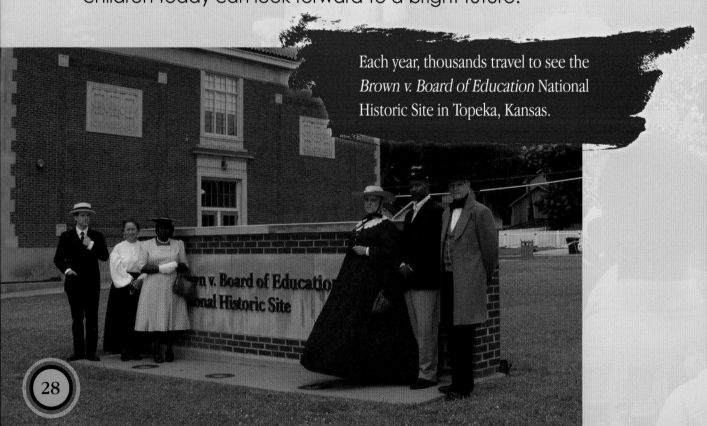

Each year, thousands travel to see the *Brown v. Board of Education* National Historic Site in Topeka, Kansas.

Equality for All

When African Americans fought for the rights of their children, they did not realize they would change history. The parents, their children, and students who make up this story were teachers, secretaries, welders, ministers, and students who simply wanted to be treated equally. If it were not for these ordinary people, education and society as we know it today might not exist. It is these people Americans should thank for winning equality for all.

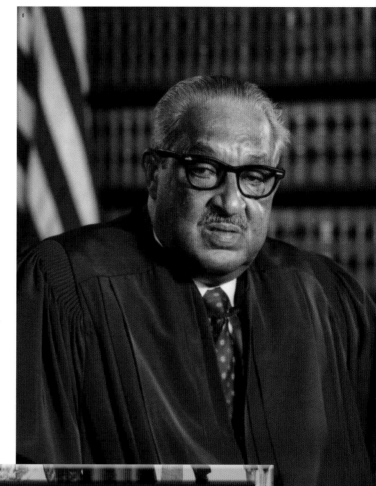

Thurgood Marshall

Thurgood Marshall (above) was the grandson of a slave. He studied at Howard University Law School and went on to work with the NAACP. Marshall was the head lawyer for the plaintiffs in *Brown v. Board of Education*. Later, he served as a judge and as the first African American Solicitor General, the lawyer who represents the US in Supreme Court cases. In 1967, President Lyndon Johnson nominated him to the US Supreme Court, and on October 2 of that year, Marshall was sworn in as its first African American justice. His story inspires people to this day.

Glossary

appeal (uh-PEEL) In law, if a court case is lost an appeal can be made to hear the case at a higher court.

Caucasian (kah-KAY-zhun) A light-skinned person of European origin.

challenge (CHA-lenj) To question the rightness of something.

chancellor (CHAN-suh-lur) A head judge.

civil rights (SIH-vul RYTS) The rights given by a government to all its citizens.

constitution (kon-stih-TOO-shun) The written laws of a country.

curriculum (kur-RIH-kyoo-lum) Courses taught at schools.

curtailed (kur-TAYLD) Shortened.

discrimination (dis-krih-muh-NAY-shun) Treating some people differently from others.

equalization (ee-kwuh-luh-ZAY-shun) To make equal.

governor (GUH-vun-ur) A person in government.

graduating (GRA-juh-wayt-ing) Finishing high school or college.

inauguration (ih-naw-gyuh-RAY-shun) An official ceremony at the start of a presidency.

integrate (IN-tuh-grayt) To bring together, to mix.

munitions (myuh-NIH-shunz) Weaponry such as swords, guns, and bullets.

National Guard (NASH-nul GARD) A US military force maintained by each state, that can be called upon by either the state or federal government.

plaintiffs (PLAYN-tifs) People who start a lawsuit.

plantations (plan-TAY-shunz) Large farms used for growing rubber, cotton, or other crops to sell.

racial (RAY-shul) To do with a race of people.

Republican (rih-PUH-blih-ken) A member of the Republican Party.

segregation (seh-gruh-GAY-shun) A system to keep white Americans and African Americans apart.

strike (STRYK) To stop work or study as a form of protest.

Supreme Court (suh-PREEM KORT) The highest court in the United States.

unconstitutional (un-kon-stih-TOO-shuh-nul) Against the written laws of a country.

violate (VY-uh-layt) To break.

Further Reading

Conaway, Judith. *Brown v. Board of Education: The Case for Integration*. Snapshots in History. Mankato, MN: Compass Point Books, 2007.

Foy, Debbie. *Civil-Rights Activists*. Black History Makers. New York: PowerKids Press, 2012.

Linde, Barbara. *Thurgood Marshall*. Civil Rights Crusaders. New York: Gareth Stevens Learning Library, 2011.

Websites

Due to the changing nature of Internet links, PowerKids Press has developed an online list of websites related to the subject of this book. This site is updated regularly. Please use this link to access the list:
www.powerkidslinks.com/wso/brown/

Index